Don't Br Wo

CW00920988

Songs and Poems

To Donnie

with love

Anne Marie Brian

Anne Marie Brian

chipmunkapublishing
the mental health publisher

Anne Marie Brian

Published by
Chipmunkapublishing
PO Box 6872
Brentwood
Essex CM13 1ZT
United Kingdom

http://www.chipmunkapublishing.com

Copyright © Anne Marie Brian 2010

Chipmunkapublishing gratefully acknowledge the support of Arts Council England.

Don't Breathe a Word

This book is dedicated to

All my friends

On the wards

And on the streets

Anne Marie Brian

Author Biography

Anne Marie Brian was born in Hammersmith, London in 1959. She was educated at a Convent school from which she was expelled at the age of 14. She did not like school much but managed to obtain a smattering of qualifications later on.

She had her first "breakdown" at the age of 26, when delirium tremens was incorrectly diagnosed as a drugs overdose, and treated with a cocktail of psychiatric medication. Her consultant psychiatrist said at the time that she would be in hospital for two years, but her parents kept her at home, and three months later, she was off all the medication and back at work.

At the age of 30, while in the middle of a degree course, Anne Marie was hospitalised, sectioned, and labelled "schizophrenic". Six months later, after her release from hospital, she stopped the injections of modecate and recovered sufficiently to work full-time, and so her consultant psychiatrist changed her diagnosis to "manic depressive".

In 1994 Anne Marie had son, Callum. Despite all the negative input from psychiatric services, who harrassed her to such an extent that she had a breakdown when seven months pregnant, she not only successfully raised Callum, but also home-educated him from the age of 7.

Anne Marie lives with Callum and her partner, Iain, in Berkshire.

Anne Marie Brian

Don't Breathe a Word

"Illness" or "Ability"? (for my doctor)

I can …

Fly like an angel

Across the sea

And love everyone

Even if they hate me

I can …

Smell the sun

On the trees

And instantly put you

At your ease

Or listen to the grass

And feel the running feet

Of ages past

I can …

Look into your eyes

And see your ancient soul

And hug you

Until you feel completely whole

I can …

Catch the moonlight

On the lake

And tangled cobwebs

Made of lace

To weave an Elfin gift for you

I can …

See the world

In a single flower

And look around

For fruit that's sour

And taste if first, so you don't thirst

I can …

Catch a rainbow

For all to see

And dance in the light

That follows me

And in my mind's eye perceive

Don't Breathe a Word

Prophets of old

In raiments of gold

I can ...

See God in the faces

Of people I meet

Especially the poor ones

On the street

And, feeling the love

They badly need

Try to protect them from

This world of greed

I can ...

Let down an onion

Into your hell

And as I chant my ancient spells

A kindly spirit

In my heart

Beckons me to take your part

I can ...

Write a Sonnet in sixty seconds

And hum a tune

Until fame beckons

Or dance in the nude

And make you laugh

Until you ache for solitude

I can …

See the face of Jesus

In an ordinary window

I can breathe

The changing seasons

Like a silver minnow

And see the world in the eye of a fly

And

Climbing higher

Walk into the sky

What am I?

To you, "Bipolar"

But, in ancient times,

perhaps,

"Mage", "Soothsayer", "Auger", "Shaman", "Prophet"

or even

"Saint"?

Born to Cry

All over the world

There are those

Beside themselves with grief

For the loss

Of someone they loved

And I don't know why

We are born to cry

In a little while

The tears wash away the pain

Like beautiful rain

But still my heart

Is empty

Where it used to be warm

At the sight of you

What am I to do

Now you are gone?

When every breath I took

Don't Breathe a Word

Was for you?

How can I pretend

My love has an end?

How can I look at our child

And not see you?

How can I believe in

The beauty of the world

If I see it without you?

You will never know

How helpless, sad,

Bereft, and mad

You left me,

How I wept

Like one born to cry

Cornwall

Sunset over the sea

Red and orange melting

On the horizon

And seagulls

The sky acrobats

Silhouetted

Black as the night that follows

And oh, the stars!

And the moonlight

Dancing on the waves

That crash

On the rocks below

Sending a spray

That makes the air

Taste so sweet and fresh

I am dizzy

And might fall

Don't Breathe a Word

It is cold now

A bitter wind

Makes me glad I am not far

From a warm bed

And as I dream

I can still hear

The Ocean, my friend

Anne Marie Brian

Don't Breathe a Word

<u>Verse 1</u>:

Sometimes I look at you

And your smile drives me crazy

I need your touch

This is not enough

I want to be your fantasy

<u>Chorus:</u>

You said to me…

Don't breathe a word of the way you feel

Even though it seems so real

I'll be there when I want to be

I won't live your fantasy

And when you need to hug me

Don't let yourself love me

Falling in love

Wasn't part of the deal

Don't breathe a word of the way you feel

Don't Breathe a Word

It's just a dream it can't be real

Verse 2:

Tonight I want your love

But I'm scared you'll back away

Your eyes meet mine

I just look down

When I want to say

"Please stay"

Verse 3:

Sometimes you say her name

And it cuts me like a knife

You don't know

I'd sell my soul

To call myself your wife

Verse 4:

Tonight we had some fun,

some laughs

But then you run for cover

I'm just a kid

With vivid dreams

I'd die to be your lover

Funny if …

Funny if …

The Earth was ruled

By a race of

Giant plants

And they liked

To put

The severed limbs

Of mammals

In glass vases …

Anne Marie Brian

Letters to a Movie Star

I want to touch your life somehow

To cause a laugh, a raised eyebrow

With clumsy prose I do intend

To amuse, not to offend

My reasons are not clear to me

You the giant, me the flea

Am I being masochistic

To try to reach my distant mystic?

The sculptured beauty of your face

Reminds me of another place

Where nature did not wear a frown

Nor the Earth her fruit disown

Then, like now, you were a teacher

You knew the worth of every creature

Now you're a star and I'm a fan

But this is not how it began

Don't Breathe a Word

So many lives, so many roles

To you I know I'm just a prole

You whose friends are movie greats

Not to mention heads of state

But when your arms enwrap a tree

That same life-force is part of me

And so, my Inca Princess, listen

To words of love so freely given

My Guitar

Brown and tan wood

Edged in black

A curvaceous woman

With a long slender neck

Six taut strings

Cheesewire sharp

Wound around white pegs

Between these

White inlay imitates ivory

Black scratchplate

On which pink butterflies float

Borders the sound hole

An open mouth

Ready to sing

Don't Breathe a Word

My Love is Unfaithful

Into my pillow I softly weep

I cannot find comfort in sleep

For,

Though my Love

Is playful, joyful,

I despair when he's unfaithful

I can smell the tempting kisses

Of this cunning liquid mistress

Coming in delicious forms, she

Seduces him

With poisons warm

That sweet lure of liquor beckons

And the first one's down in seconds

And, though he swears he'll give her up

There's always one more little sup

I cannot kill her with a sword

Nor with a thousand chosen words

Her magic's of a deadly kind

The spells she weaves will drive him blindly to – oblivion!

While he's deaf to my cries

And the tears in my eyes

He mistakes for laughter

Don't Breathe a Word

Lynstock Crescent

Oh no oh no they've sold Lynstock Crescent

The place where as a boy I chased a pheasant

Into the house where my Auntie screamed,

"Get that bird out of here!" while I beamed

Mischievously!

No more holidays in Nethy Bridge

Where we'd be eaten alive by the midge

And run around like a pack of wild things

And jump on tomatoes found in the fridge

Quite happily!

A house full of laughter and children and dogs

And jumbled-up coats and hats filled with frogs

With tatties and neeps and haggis for tea

Or some bit of venison my Dad got for free

Naughtily!

We made a camp, we had a war,

We ran around, then ran some more

Anne Marie Brian

We'd feast on bread and jam and Spam

(Which in those days was a tin of ham)

Deliciously!

There was me and Gary that Summers' day

Hiding in the tent right where there lay

A huge cherry cake for all to see

The prize to have later with a cup of tea

So temptingly!

We ran off and scoffed it all

The sponge, the cherries, the icing, more

Than we could comfortably eat

But we ate up all this lovely treat

Most wickedly!

We played a game, we kicked a ball

We were the ones who could not fall

When we jumped and climbed the trees

And chased away the angry bees

Exuberantly!

Don't Breathe a Word

How did this ever come to pass?

Can it be true? They've stolen my past! And –

Somebody else lives in the house on the end

Where us kids would drive you around the bend

Unthinkable!

Outcast

I am an Outcast

From across the sea

When I walk into danger

No-one follows me

I am an Outcast

With no family tree

To you I'm just a stranger

With no history

I am an Outcast

No-one knows my name

Will you plead my case

Or let me die of shame?

I am an Outcast

Just a picture in a frame

Will you ever see

That you and I are just the same?

I am an Outcast

Don't Breathe a Word

But will you call me "Brother"?

I have a heart as red as yours

But I can't buy another

I am an Outcast

A slave to circumstances

Will you reach out to me

Or, rewriting history

Leave me to my chances?

I am an Outcast

No friends to call upon

When dragons breathe fire

And take away my all

I am an Outcast

Will you watch me fall

Upon my funeral pyre

And, with tearless eyes

Condemn me to eternity, in Thrall?

I am an Outcast

I do not ask for much

Anne Marie Brian

Some chickens or a cow

Strong children and a leak-proof hut

I am an Outcast

I am too proud to beg

But will you let me have enough

To keep my head

Or sell me guns

To fight your wars?

Pheasants in Spring

He struts

Puffs out his chest

Fans his feathers

Like a fighting cock

Dressed to impress

In speckled brown and red

His blue head hooded

Like a bird of prey

He circles his dowdy mate

She darts away

He corners her

She protests

With a grinding cluck

Like a faulty starter motor

She makes her escape

Only to let him catch her

Again and again

Anne Marie Brian

Pillow Talk

Verse 1:

It's 3am and I can't sleep

My mind's made up, my emotions are spent

I know I said I'd always love you

But now your kiss is the kiss of death

Chorus:

Pillow talking I was walking on air

Running my fingers through your hair

Pillow talking I was walking on air

But now it's the end of this love affair

It's the end of this love affair

Verse 2:

It's 3 am and you're sleeping

I look at you and wish you were dead

Too many lies, too many cries

So when you wake,

Don't Breathe a Word

You'll find me gone

Verse 3:

It's 3am and I'm on my way

You could never beg me to stay

The pillow talks and that's a shame

I know I'll never come this way again

Anne Marie Brian

Pwyll Y Gaseg - My Sister Margaret's Home

Nappies flying

Breeze drying

A rabbit, hopping

Goats bleat and butt and chew

Tractor humming

Rosie running, sheepishly

Green hills

A buzzard, circling

Orchids hide

A forest beckons

Cows graze distantly, black and white

Bluebells blossom

Yellow gorse smells of coconut

Mushrooms grow, sweet

Children laugh, giggle, play, push, swing, bat, run, shout, tumble

Black cat eyes a Bantam

Cocks doodle-do

Don't Breathe a Word

Grass soft, green, lush

Flowers purple

Rain tumbling

Storm brewing

Stars twinkling

Inside

Washed clothes

Herbs and spices

Home-baked bread

Wood stove glows, welcoming

Quarry tiles, browny red

Books in a jumble

Coats on hooks

Boots in porch

A comfort blanket, draped

Cutlery, crockery, goat's milk, cheese

Coffee brewing

Margaret mothers

Richard cuddles

Baby snuggles

Don't Breathe a Word

Shot Away

<u>Spoken</u>:

Come along, come along to Schuster Towers

Where Longface nurtures us like flowers

Like specimens we are to him

Drugged to the hilt

On just a whim

<u>Chorus</u>:

They got me shot away – hey hey hey

They got me shot away – hey hey hey

They got me shot away – hey hey hey

They got me shot away – hey hey hey

<u>Verse 1</u>:

The gangster's trying to get me out

My mother comes, I scream and shout

All the patients have mobile phones

I'm driven mad by ringing tones

Verse 2:

Please fix these questions in my brain

Why do they say that I'm insane?

My anorexic friend, fighting jealousy

Leaves chocolate on my pillow, for free

Verse 3:

My Dad he says I drive him mad

He cannot see me and I'm glad

The fire alarm will make us deaf

And if we're bored we'll eat the Chef

Verse 4:

The nurses they all laugh at me

They will never set me free

There's too much noise to get bed rest

So Zopichlone will fill my nest

Verse 5:

There's pervy people all around

Don't Breathe a Word

They make me jump with sudden sounds

The tattooed man he fancies me

He gives false clues and confuses me

Verse 6:

And all I hear is jangley keys

The Chinese man will marry me

If he likes the songs I sing

While we wait for toast to ping

Verse 7:

My heart is pounding under the strain

Another shot to kill the brain

I get injected in my bed

When I wake up I'm just as dead

Don't set us free, don't set us free

We must preserve – our society's ILLUSION OF SANITY

So glad it's raining

I am so glad it's raining

To hide my tears

I came home and thought of you

And everything you put me through

And it did not seem fair

The way you gently touched my hair

And whispered that you loved me

When all along you wanted

Someone else

I am so glad it's raining

To hide my fears

I came home and buried myself

In pillows that were wet with tears

I have been known to write a sonnet

But you only wanted someone to pose on your bonnet

You said that I was beautiful

But all your feelings were dishonest

Don't Breathe a Word

I am so glad it's raining

To hide my weakness

Like a fool I fell for you

You didn't speak one word that was true

So here I am still waiting

And the phone will not ring

What sorrow love can bring

What a shame you cannot die

Of a broken heart

I am so glad it's raining

You never gave me a second thought

It was all pain and misery that you brought

With your blue-eyed smile

I will think of you for a while

The way you took me on the sofa

And I think even you might be glad to know

I did it because I loved you so

Anne Marie Brian

Song for Donnie Munro

Donnie Munro - you are so handsome

For time with you I would pay a King's ransom

Donnie Munro - you are so Scottish

I guess that's because you wouldn't be English!

Donnie Munro – when you're on the stage

My heart's on fire and I'll never age

Donnie Munro – when you put on a show

When it comes to the end, I don't want to go

Donnie Munro – when you speak, it's like music,

Your voice is so soft, and Scottish, and soothing

I will never forget your beautiful words

And beautiful heart, and beautiful soul

Donnie, to me, you will never grow old

Donnie Munro, well, what can I say?

I wish you were mine, just for a day!

Let me explain …

Donnie Munro, you were so polite,

Don't Breathe a Word

When I ran to you, and gave you a fright

I was on holiday on the Isle of Skye

I went that far North, I don't really know why

Then I remembered it was Runrig's home

The band I so loved when a student "in Rome"

I played all their songs at a deafening level

Just so all my friends would call me a Rebel:

The drums and the pipes, the accordion, loud

No wonder these Scottish boys were so proud

I loved the poems, the singing, the songs

I would listen so avidly, all day long

Then,

Terrible news!

Donnie was leaving!

I cried and cried, my heart was heaving

How could he, I thought, after all we'd be through?

Was it the end of the band, could this really be true?

Now we have found out, and it's a joy to behold,

That Donnie writes songs worth his weight in gold

With beautiful words and beautiful melodies,

His pictures and tunes, they really do stand at ease

Next to the work of Burns and Scott,

And Shelley and Keats and all that lot!

Your life's work, is your language to preserve

The English had such a monstrous nerve

To try to break Scotland's heart and culture

You should have picked over

England's wicked bones like vultures

This is the history they hid from me at school

I had to grow up to learn the truth

And although I am English, I am so touched by your story

The battles, the blood, the fame and the glory

That,

I have just one wish for my life, today

And that's to live North of the Border one beautiful day.

Now I must go and make a cup of tea

And hope that you will like my poetry

Don't Breathe a Word

I know you will be embarrassed and shy

Because you are just that kind of guy

Donnie, you mean so much to me

Your poems and songs, they set me free,

Just one more thing,

Will you marry me?

Anne Marie Brian

Song for Mair (Child of the Sun)

<u>Verse 1</u>:

Here you are in the world

A beautiful girl!

Your heart is a diamond

Your soul, a pearl

You sing happy songs

Which make things so clear

Now we know we belong

Right here

<u>Verse 2</u>:

The faint sounds of the birds

Beckon me to the dawn

The sun kisses the crops

As they dance by the lawn

I look for you, Lord

In the eyes of my child

And find You are there

Don't Breathe a Word

Once again

<u>Verse 3</u>:

It's not raining today

At my Welsh hillside home

My goats are in kid

Washing's dry as a bone

I walk hand in hand

With the Lord as I sow

Seeds of love and of hope

All around

<u>Verse 4</u>:

Will you please tell me, Lord

If I did the right things?

If I sang the right songs,

Your message to bring?

Did I carve out my life

With carpenter's hands?

Will you still take me home

When I'm called?

<u>Chorus:</u>

Child of the sun

Don't you know your life

Has just begun?   (4 times)

Don't Breathe a Word

The Ballad of Graham Ballantyne

Chorus:

Oh Graham Ballantyne

I did not know you all that well

But when you get to heaven

Will you come back for me?

Verse 1:

You were not so old when I met you

The ward's surroundings made you blue

You were too drugged to feel alive

You said it was a struggle to survive

Verse 2:

You took my hand, you were my friend

You could have lived right to the end

But a nurse she said a cruel word

And made you cry – I overheard

Verse 3:

You had a smile that made me laugh

But the changing memories of your past

Were written on the walls that day

You chose to take your life away

Verse 4:

Farewell my man, my gentle knight

Who, in the end, gave up the fight

You had no family to wish you well

And so the nurses made it hell

Verse 5:

Your tattered clothes were all I saw

As nurses swarmed around your door

I guessed you'd gone down to the tracks

And you were never coming back

Don't Breathe a Word

The Dream

Tumbling, tumbling

Never touching the ground

But flirting with it

I fly, I float

With ease

Up, up into Space now –

I am in a cube

Of glass

Someone says, "Look at the stars –

The bright souls of the departed!"

The sky is blood red

We are cold and wet

We find shelter in a cave

Etched in the stone wall

Ancient graffiti warns, "Beware!"

I am driving a car

Full of giggly people

One by one they go

I am left

With a knot in my stomach

An exam tomorrow

And I am unprepared

At College now

But it's work

Outside, the sky is perfect

Baby blue

I gaze longingly across the park

Martin finds and eats my lunch,

Ham and pickle sandwiches

"I'm starving!" he says

"Two days to Giro day

And no food in the house!"

I sympathise

As usual

To Be Young

Mum you're so sweet

In your clothes so neat

You twirl and dance

And dream of Romance

Mum you're so young

You like to have fun

You're the Belle of the Ball

Down the local dance hall

Mum when I watch you

Twirl skip and tango

My heart overflows

It's the end of my "lows"

I wish we could stay

For ever and a day

And Tango like mad

And still cuddle Dad

Anne Marie Brian

Mum, I am like you

I have lots of dreams, too

I want to have artists

Admire what I try to do

But most of all, Mum

Before we are done

I wish just to love you

And hold you when you're blue

Mum you have beauty

That's timeless as Torquay

Where you go for your hols

And you all softly stroll

Down to the dance floor

To dream of Romance

And another chance – to be young

Don't Breathe a Word

Turkish Delight

<u>Verse 1</u>:

In my dreams your eyes are

Burning in the dark

With poison claws upon my back

You make your mark

So exotic, so mysterious

Your charms drive me delirious

And all I ever wanted was the secrets of your heart

<u>Chorus:</u>

You're my Turkish Delight, demon of the night

Your smile comes back to me

Your dagger cloaked in mystery

You are my naked fantasy

My Turkish Delight

<u>Verse 2</u>:

Above the gates of hell

A devil wrote your name

And then you came to me

To play your evil game

You trapped and made a slave of me

A captive of your treachery

And now my life is history

But still you feel no shame

Verse 3:

You flashed your killer smile

And walked out of my life

A thousand deaths I died

At the twist of that knife

Your power terrified me

Satisfied me

Now it blinds me

All I see is Turkish Dreams,

Your face, your laugh, your light

Don't Breathe a Word

<u>Verse 4</u>:

You still hold my life

In your olive-skinned hand

I am but a shell, an empty shadow,

The damned

Eastern promises broken

Forgotten words of love softly spoken

You slip through my fingers

Like a grain of sand

What harm could it do?

Every time I say "I love you"

It hurts me inside

The way you just kiss me

But never reply

Why is it so hard for you

To say you love me too?

What has the past done to you?

If I said this was "Goodbye"

Would it make you cry?

Would you wish you'd said those words

I long to hear?

Don't say it to please me

That would never do

I have to know your feelings are true

You say you'll try to show me

How deep your feelings go

Don't Breathe a Word

But I can't wait forever

I have to know

And if you could say it before

It shows you loved her more

What harm could it do to say "I love you"?

I don't like Psychiatrists

I don't like Psychiatrists

Because they've got no bones

I don't like Glaxo Smith Klein

Coz they like to keep you stoned

I don't like Psychiatrists

Because they've got no souls

I'd like to blow up Bayer-UK

For making me a zombie clone

I don't like Psychiatrists

Because they are all mad

They lock us in together

Then wonder why we're sad

I don't like Psychiatrists

They stroke their greying beards

Make snap decisions about my life

As if it's me that's weird

Don't Breathe a Word

I don't like Psychiatrists

They always scratch their heads

When walking 'round the ward at night

Inspecting us in bed

I don't like Psychiatrists

They drive us all insane

They like to think they're better

Coz they have a boring brain

I don't like Psychiatrists

They always tut and moan

And say I have to stay inside

When I just want to go home

I don't like Psychiatrists

They like to joke and laugh

Together after a long day

Of reaping up the past

I don't like Psychiatrists

I don't see why I should

Anne Marie Brian

Zombie round on drugs all day

Which are "for my own good"

I don't like Psychiatrists

Because they make me stay

In their hell until I'm "well"

Or less mad in their opinionated way

I don't like Psychiatrists

And now I'll tell you why

They think it is a mortal sin

To see God in the sky

I don't like Psychiatrists

Because they think they're always right

They sit around and drink some tea

Make lots of money from our misery

I don't like Psychiatrists – who would?

Don't Breathe a Word

My Scottish Isle

Pink sky promises later sun

Rainbows light up our way

As muddy tracks to distant mountains beckon

Red squirrels dart and play

Banana seals laze in the bay

Enjoying their fame

Music is everywhere

The birds sing happily

Like the people here

We cannot take our eyes

Off the skyline –

The mountains are so beautiful -

They fill with tears

"We are in Paradise!"

A distant chainsaw hums

Someone is making sculptures in wood

Living their dream

Anne Marie Brian

The wind rustles the trees

A buzzard hovers

I rush for my camera

With Runrig on my mind

Making me think of Scotland's history

A dog barks hugely

It is Ronach! We hug him, we love him

Blue skies, grey skies

Marjorie's fantastic soup

Warms us

Rain and sunshine in equal measures

Rain that tastes as sweet

As the crystal clear burn water

Cool and refreshing

Like the air

The burns twinkle and flow

Down to the sea

Where the sand is so soft

I could sleep all day

Don't Breathe a Word

This island has stolen my heart

And I would almost give my soul

To stay forever

Anne Marie Brian

I Am Home

Get up six O'clock

Get a fizz from the Colgate

Eat some

Crunchy chewy bits and pieces

At the bus stop seven O'clock

Get a buzz from the nicotine

Rain's pouring down again

Swishy swashy cars

Go by

Bus driver looks so mean!

He's fat and coughs and nods

No room to sit down

All the people frown

Ah well,

Jack Kerouac in my pocket

Making me feel

Part of something good

Don't Breathe a Word

Get to work

Grey factory gates open

I can make a lot of shower hoses today

Get my pay, get some beer

And go down to the town

Watch those crazy fools drive around

Pub lights

Warm and beckoning

My day of reckoning

Is far, far away

Memories stealing into my vodka

Like the kisses of a thousand boys

I would rather forget

I will beat them all yet

But not today

I stagger and sway

Lipstick smeared all over my face

Not a trace of love here

Only bitter vultures

Coming in for the kill

They don't know or care

About my gifts

They just want my lemon thighs

I apologise and exit, stage left

Waiting for a taxi now

There are scuffles in the queue

Like angry bears

They growl and brawl

Taxi driver smokes

I choke again on memories

As we drive through the town

Every street corner

Holds the past

I want to forget

At last,

A funny story later

I am Home

Don't Breathe a Word

But, Mr Psychosis … What is it Like?

I am in a movie

With dazzling special effects

I live in a movie

But I have no script

I am not human

And my eyes are cameras

The scientists that made me

Can see what I see

And read my every thought

I want to run away

From myself

I walk five miles

Along the edge of a motorway

My heavy bag

Of evidence

Weighing me down

Humans are made into Androids

Anne Marie Brian

At the hospital

I have to tell someone!

I am locked in a police cell

For seven hours

If I tell them my name

I will be killed

I will be ashes on the floor

Burned and decapitated

Or gassed with poison

The policemen laugh

Long and loud

At what I think is the Truth

One of them looks

Like a young Richard Burton

He was on the telly this morning

Is he a robot too?

I am a good robot

I want to help the humans

But I cannot help but weep

Don't Breathe a Word

Because a robot would not have an immortal soul

My home town

Is a concrete island

Floating in the English channel

Hitler won the war

And he wants me dead

And so does Tony Blair

In London

I wander the streets

I have no glasses

I have thrown them away

Because they contain transmitters

So I cannot see

I am a Princess too

Walt Disney is my father

I have to die to save Diana

Because my name is Die-Anna

In a police car now

Heading for home

A silver blue knight

On a beautiful white charger

Overtakes us

In hospital

I scream and scream

My blood

Is on fire

An Indian chief

In full ceremonial dress

Melts out of a wall

Suddenly -

I am no longer afraid!

I am an Angel

I lie on my bed

And listen to the rhythmic

Beat of my wings

I feel the soft breeze they make

Against my face

I am at peace

Don't Breathe a Word

I am held by God

If I died it would not matter

As it is a bridge to heaven

I have been in a war

Of my own creation

Now let me die

In peace

Angel

I am an Angel

Who came to Earth

Won't somebody help me

Find my way back to heaven?

Jimi Hendrix is my brother

Janis Joplin is my sister

J F Kennedy is my father

John Lennon is my lover

Marilyn Munro is my sister

Martin Luther King is my brother

Jesus is my father

Krishna is my lover

Mother Theresa is my saviour

Mary is my Mother

Diana is my sister

Michael Jackson is my lover

Ghandi is my salvation

Don't Breathe a Word

Mohammed is my brother

Yahweh walks beside me

I am an Angel

Who came to Earth

Won't somebody

Help me find my way

Back to heaven?

My Garden

An oak on the horizon

And daffodils, sunshine yellow

Whirlygigs for washing

Mock trees in metal and plastic

A dove lands in the oak

Joining its mate

Over the fence

A playground – happy shrieks

Burst the silence

More knotty trees

Trunks thinning

To the tips of branches

They are grey

But brightened by green ivy

A thrush scurries

Then is still as stone

A black rook flies across

Don't Breathe a Word

Twig in beak

There are diamonds in the mud

A magpie scoots by

In smart sailor suit

Blue and black and white

The blue sky fades

To white and grey

The clouds bring sudden rain

Flecks of water dance

Like insects in the wind

Nicotine and Alcohol

I know some faithless people

They live quite close to me

They think that love is made

In a factory

I know some faithless people

Who love by giving things

Don't they know that God exists

And angels do have wings?

I know some faithless people

Who get their babies dunked

Then go home, drown their joys

In whatever gets them drunk

I know some faithless people

Who will get married in a church

Then go home, swear and swagger

And never search

For more meaning in their lives

Don't Breathe a Word

Spirituality

Sets you free

It's so much better

Than the drugs they crave

Although they are not illegal

Nicotine and alcohol

Are a deadly combination

For the health of our nation

Rosalie

Oh Rosalie

You just wanted

To have a baby

But they said

You were not fit

To nurse a child

And feel complete

Oh Rosalie

You just wanted

To have a baby

But they said

That you were lazy

In your gown

All stained with gravy

Oh Rosalie

They said your dream

Don't Breathe a Word

Of a lovely home

A baby of

Your very own

Was too much

For a girl to ask

In view of things

Now in the past

Oh Rosalie

They said you'd have

A dog, a bone

A big house

And a mobile phone

But you could

Never, ever have

A baby of your very own

Oh Rosalie

You just wanted

To have a baby

I could see

You weren't that crazy

You just needed

A good man, maybe

Oh Rosalie

You just wanted

To have a baby

But they said

You were too ill

And made you take

The bitter pill

Oh Rosalie

You just chose

Her lovely name

Born in spite

Of their tutting shame

She is in the world forever now

You're the best Mum

Don't Breathe a Word

I've ever known

And no-one can take her away

Rosalie

Song for Michael

A lovely boy

A beautiful boy

A voice so clear and high and pure

Feet that danced

While he laughed

So demure

Singing songs to change the world

Telling us

To all link arms

And protest for peaceful

Change in our lives

Like Diana he was Dangerous

To those who would lie

To babes in the womb

He was tortured by people

He thought he could trust

When he was only trying

Don't Breathe a Word

To help all of us

A beautiful boy

An innocent boy

Born to a Dad who used him for money

A beautiful boy

A beautiful man

We'll never see the like again

The way he died

It was not funny

Devoured by the Press

Who twisted his words of honey

A lonely boy

A special man

Singing his songs

Of love and hope

A beautiful man

A friendless man

Drugged every day

With evil dope

An innocent man

A doting father

Twisted by Paparazzi

Upon a rope

A beautiful boy

An innocent boy

The brightest star

We'll ever know

A beautiful boy

A beautiful man

His only crime was to trust

Those who go

To great lengths

To destroy

What is pure and honest

A twenty two million dollar lie

Sealed his fate

A lonely boy

A special man

Don't Breathe a Word

Watch him move

Watch him sing

He is the King

His melodies will live forever

While the surgeons

Who thought they were so clever

Will rot in Hell

Anne Marie Brian

Television

Switch me off?

Don't you dare!

I will make you stare and stare

I will tell you what to think

And what and when to drink

Desensitized to foreign news

You will watch me

Until you snooze

Switch me off?

See if you can!

You will be

My biggest fan

I will make you dream all day

Of things I make you

Want to say

Switch me off?

Not a chance!

Don't Breathe a Word

Just sit still and see romance

And watch the lovely people play

With sun and dolphins in the bay

Switch me off?

Not today!

I will always have my say

Watch the people

Jump through hoops

They're so glam

With perfect boobs

Switch me off?

You see, you can't!

You just want to laugh and laugh

But I am not really funny

I just make your life seem sunny

Switch me off?

I'd like to see you try!

When you live in tiny flats

Without TV you'd just go bats

Anne Marie Brian

But are your teeth white enough?

Is the chocolate really lush?

Switch me off?

I don't think so

We are the people you

Should Co-Co

We are the people

Put in charge

You are just

A flea at large

Switch me off?

You don't want to

I'll keep up with the main events

Baby born inside a festival tent

Man killed for being

Much too intense

Switch me off?

But I'm your keeper

Starting off with your Blue Peter

Don't Breathe a Word

I am part of your History

There is no mystery

Why I am in your lives

The Smellytubbies

In their hives

With telly on their tummies

Will make you dream of bunnies

The chosen ones

All teeth and bums

Will make you feel

That you are dumb

Will make you feel that you are fat

Until you opt

For retail therapy

White teeth plastic lips shiny hair sexy voice foreign accent pink top blue film

I wish she was my wife

I wish I had her life

Cheesy grin grey suit purple tie blond locks fake tan

Anne Marie Brian

I wish he was my man

I must write lots of fan mail

Turn me on

Take a look

You are a fish upon my hook

I'll get you stoned

Then let you see

Pictures of the world for free

Switch me off?

Well you could try, but

You must die

Believing the lie

Don't Breathe a Word

Hey, Nursey!

Hey, Nursey!

Why are you so evil?

Is it because you look like a weevil?

Why do you do that job?

It's so you can see my jeans ripped off while I sob

Then sidle up to me and whisper "I was there, with the rest of the mob"

What exactly do you see

In working here if you love to loathe me?

With no compassion in your bones

You pick on vulnerable, crazy, wild-eyed me

To mentally unclothe

Hey, Nursey!

Why do you want to torture me

And make decisions so cruelly?

You know we're all scared to complain

In case we're on the ward again

How do you actually sleep at night

Knowing your talon nails gave me a fright?

You must be a closet Lezzie

I don't mind gays

But I don't really want to be your Christmas pressie

Hey, Nursey!

To compensate for your low pay

You love to decide whether I must stay

Then you pick a casual, cruel word

You know will not be overheard

When I was writhing on the floor

I heard you whisper "What a WHORE!"

Hey Nursey!

Desensitized, you laugh at me

"I need a hug" "DON'T BOTHER ME!"

At night you sleep while being paid

And if you can't, get in a rage -

"TAKE THIS PILL AND GO TO SLEEP

Don't Breathe a Word

OR I'LL GIVE YOU A REAL REASON TO WEEP!"

Hey Nursey!

Unlike me, you can go home

And leave us here inside the snow dome

You like to read the paper on duty, undisturbed

And feel at peace and unperturbed

While for sport you carefully scheme

Of ways to pick on Tim and Jean

Hey Nursey!

I do not wish to appear rude

But this antibiotic should be taken with food

Don't tell me to do some "Penance"

As if you care tuppence

About my immortal soul

You'll get an 'A' for that essay

But I would like to ask you -

How do you spend a lifetime in the study

Of the human race

Only to get it so wrong?

Don't Breathe a Word

Freedom (for Pat)

My Harley

Shakes into life

Like a wet dog

Oil burning smells

Reach my nostrils

My boots are black leather

My feet are hot in the sun

But when we get going

The air smells fresh in my helmet

We zip along

Leaning low

Along the country lanes

My visor is splattered with insects

We're on the main road now

Spotlights shine on windows

Glinting cars shine red white and blue

Silver streaks whiz by - other bikers too fast to wave

A silver blue camper

A tree surgeon's van

A red bus stop

A red car

Red berries on a Rowan tree

A green pub with flags

Says COURAGE! PRICE DROP!

A lawn mower with an orange

Light on top

Trundles along

Smelling of cut grass

There is a high wall with barbed wire and CCTV

What secrets are within?

Dappled shade flickers

Yellow bollards glow like daytime ghosts

A roundabout comes up suddenly

I slow down into third - second - first

There is an 'M' sign for MacDonald's - things that make you go – BLEAGH!

Don't Breathe a Word

Then an Airport sign

Super Shell we can be sure of

A blonde in jeans

An old man in a cap

A 'P' for parking sign

(As a child, it meant 'P' for a pee)

Lorries are parked tidily

I speed along now

Up into fourth, then fifth

Past fields of ripe strawberries

PICK YOUR OWN

Esso up ahead - Esso blue

A field of corn ripples in the breeze

Pink and yellow petunias float in hanging baskets

A deer sign, black and red

(I hope I do not hit one)

NO ROAD MARKINGS

Oh this will be fun!

I weave and dodge between cars with ease

Then accelerate away

Lean left for a bend

Lean right

Green yellow white red cars, I overtake

Pooh! A smell of cows!

Pooh! A smell of pigs!

Zip zip zip zip - four cars all black overtake me -

Late for a funeral?

A silver blue jeep comes a bit too close

Surging with adrenalin I accelerate out of danger

Silver birch trees in green summer finery

Salute me as I travel past

Vast houses I will never be rich enough to buy

Brown campsite signs

Invite me to stay

A family all dressed in white

Like the Ski advert

Are on a hike, with a map, they laugh and play

The white line down the middle

Don't Breathe a Word

Has dead cats' eyes

On the horizon

There is a church spire, pointing to God

The clouds darken

Rain pitter patters

On my visor

Tyre rubber mixes with rain on the road

I know I could slip, but I am brave

I am young, I will never die

Cars with alien eyes approach

Daytime lights dazzle in the greying mist

I have to stop

In my hot crash helmet, my temple throbs

I am breathing exhaust fumes

Like the children in Bratislava

But I am young

I will breathe forever

There is an ambulance in front -

Somebody being born, or somebody dying?

Anne Marie Brian

I am flying past them all now

Past brown twisted oak ash birch

And a bridge over a railway that was ditched by Beeching

We eat up the roads

Get past all the jams with a wave

Have a pit-stop

Hot tea from a flask

Then my hand's back on the throttle

My toe on the brake

If you are posh you can ride a horse

But my bike is everything to me

I lovingly polish all the chrome

Touch up the rust

Adjust the gap on the spark plugs

Check the tyres for bits of stone

Because a puncture

Could throw me off

I have tasted freedom

Don't Breathe a Word

It tasted good

Her Life

An elderly lady

On her own, on the ward

Counting out her change

Though she's got no-one to phone

Her hands are shaking

Her eyes are wide and scared

She tells the same story again and again

To anyone who will listen

They took away her house

Now she's got nowhere to go

Her man is in his grave

She smiles fondly, and shows me a faded photo

Of a handsome young man in army uniform

"That's my Joe", she says, "We never had children, I couldn't, you see".

She starts to cry, and takes a hanky out of her pocket to dab her eyes

"I hate this place", she says

Don't Breathe a Word

She wanted to be free for just a moment

And walk barefoot on the grass

But the nurses told her off

And made her come inside

The ward is hot, stifling

With all the windows locked on a summer's evening

If only I could carry her away to her childhood

When she ran barefoot in the meadows of her youth

Before the electric shocks melted her memories

And left an empty shell to fill

With the thick drip of despair

It could be heaven in here, but really it's each person's personal hell

"I want to go home", she says

But she wants more than that

She wants to go back in time

To when she and Joe had their life

She made curtains for their home on a sewing machine that she turned by hand

Joe made a shed and a run to house a few chickens

Anne Marie Brian

They both liked gardening, him vegetables and her, flowers

Later on, he got interested in racing pigeons, which she only tolerated

She did not like them pooing on the washing

When he retired from the Electricity Board, for whom he used to read meters

They bought their first ever brand new car

He liked a pipe and sometimes cigarettes,

He got hooked when they were given free to the troops

That's what killed him

He was so looking forward to retirement, and then he only had five and a half years

She used to make bramble jelly in the autumn, and apple sauce with apples from their tree

She was a compulsive knitter, and Joe always wore his sweaters with pride

She could knit one up in a few days without even looking at the pattern

She only ever worked part-time, in a paper shop just around the corner

She never learned to drive

They didn't really have a lot of friends

Don't Breathe a Word

But they went on nice holidays in a caravan by the sea
at Weymouth

"Where have the years gone?"

"Let's get a cup of tea", I suggest

And, arm in arm

We march defiantly to the kitchen

Even though we should be in bed

And all the lights are off

"Milk and sugar?"

"Just milk, please. Thank you, you are a dear. Will you
stay up with me for a bit?

Only the long corridor to my bed

Scares me."

Anne Marie Brian

Wolf

Her amber eyes

Fix on mine

My soul is read

In an instant

The Alpha female

Is sleek as silk in her movements

Her black fur ruffles in the wild summer wind

She submits only

To the Alpha male

And then

Only if she wants to

Her long expressive tail

Is up as I approach

So I know I must submit

Her perfect white teeth

Grin into a growl

Why do we persecute her?

Don't Breathe a Word

She reminds us of our ancient past

In the Wilderness

We were friends and allies then

We shared the same fire

Hunted the same prey

Grew in mutual respect

Now we have tamed her

And made her

Dacshund, Rotweiler, Chihuahua, Shih Tzu, St Bernard,
Alsatian, Poodle, Spaniel, Labrador ...

And then I see the cubs

They are so dear

I could cuddle them for all eternity

They are hungry now

She dozes as they drink

Then licks and tends them

My camera records every intimate moment

But we have been followed ...

A rifle crack

Anne Marie Brian

Rents the blood-red sky

Punctures the silence

Tears my heart

Birds fly in fear

She goes down, bleeding

I run to her, too late, too late

She trusted me, and I have brought Death

I call it Murder

To make a hunter's trophy

Of my graceful, beautiful sister

They will kill the cubs or sell them to a zoo

Her pelt will adorn a fireplace

We are custodians of this Earth

And we were not given dominion over all living creatures

To abuse them so cruelly

We are the gardeners,

We should still be in Eden

But we have become the evil destroyers

I wish humans would die out

Don't Breathe a Word

To give this beautiful home planet

A chance to recover from our greed

Lightning Source UK Ltd.
Milton Keynes UK
31 July 2010

157637UK00002B/1/P